JOHN THOMPSON RECITAL SERIES

Intermediate to Advanced

WALTZES

6 GREAT ARRANGEMENTS BY JOHN THOMPSON

ISBN 978-1-4803-9968-6

Exclusively Distributed By

HAL•LEONARD®
CORPORATION
7777 W. Bluemound Rd. P.O. Box 13819
Milwaukee, Wisconsin 53213

Visit Hal Leonard Online at
www.halleonard.com

Contents

Dark Eyes

Russian Folksong
Arranged by John Thompson

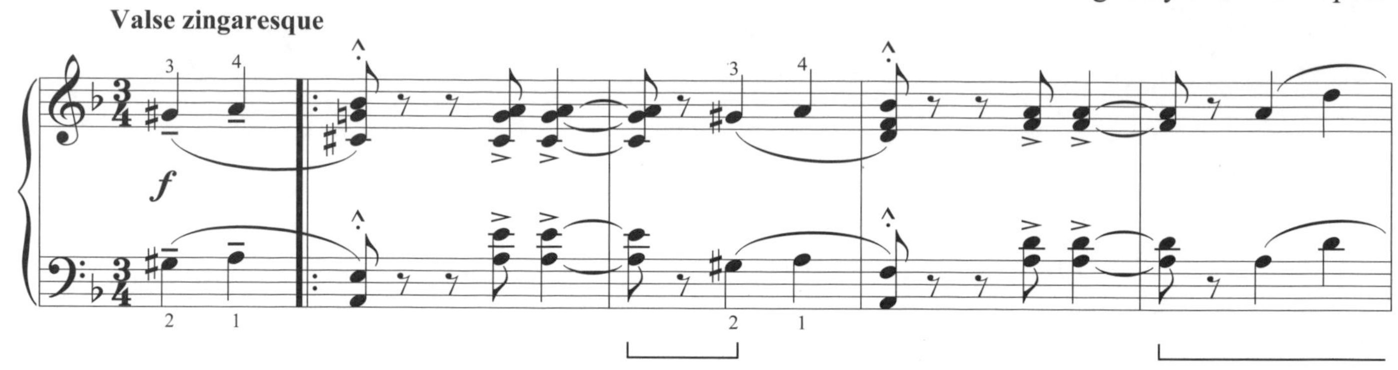

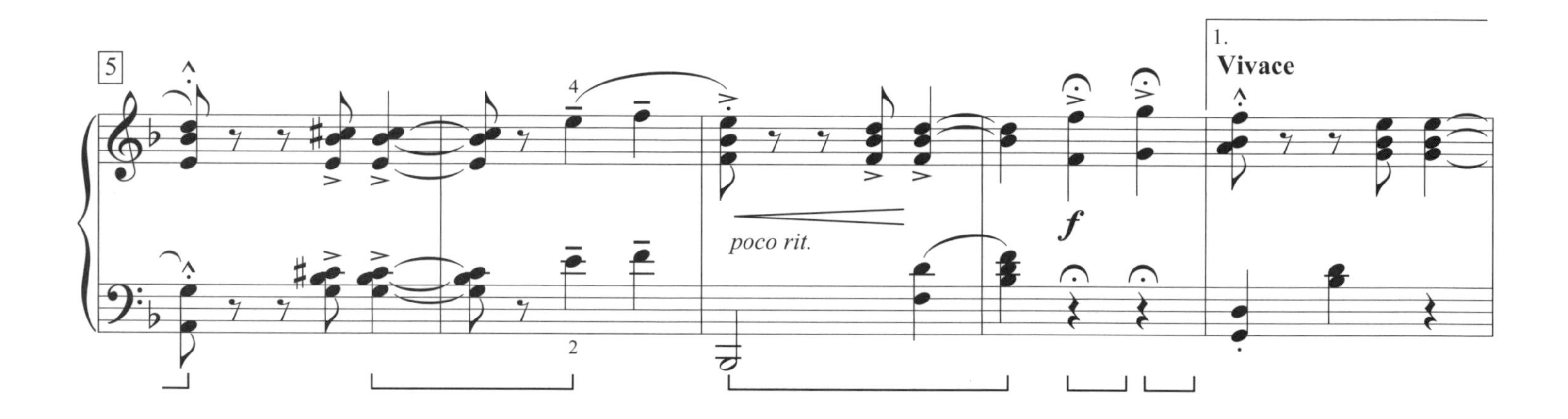

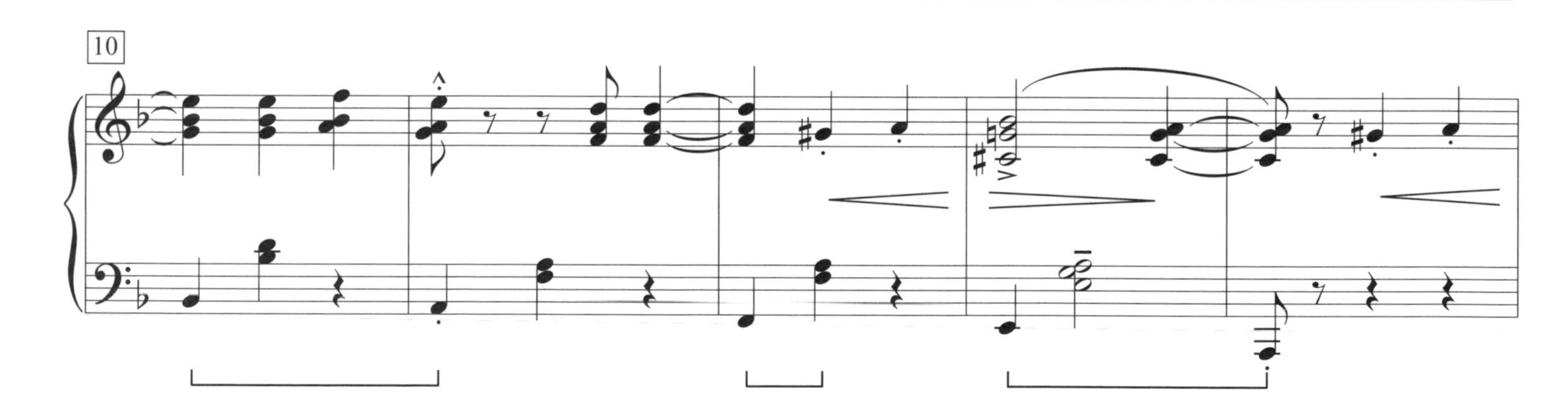

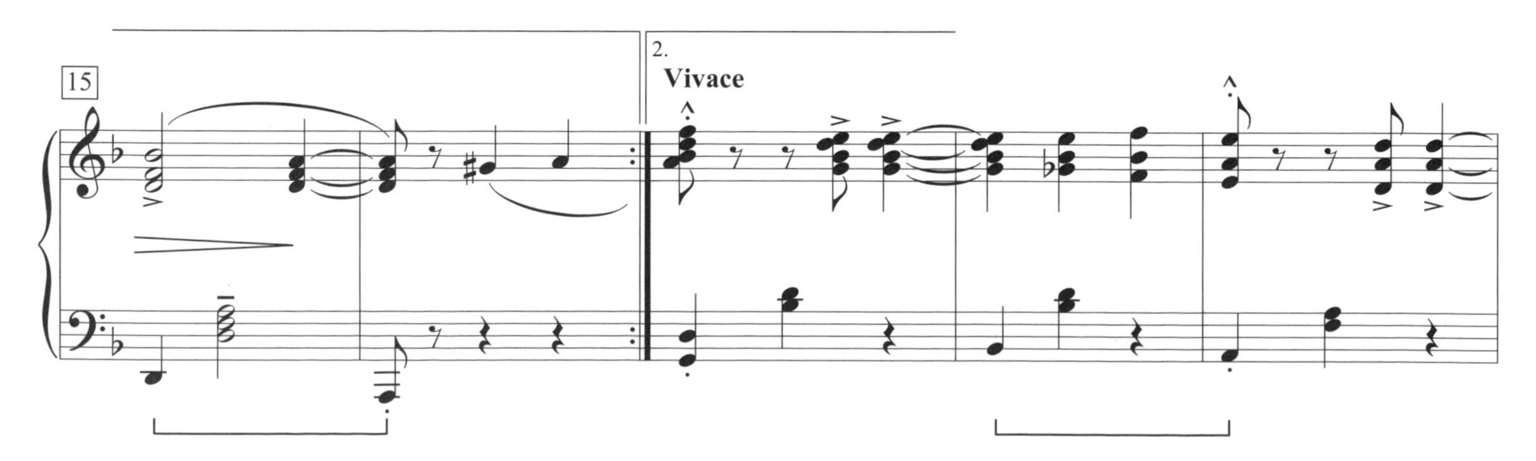

20
sfz
pp
Poco più lento
25
espressivo
31
37
mf
43
f
ff

sfz
ff
sfz
p
pp
L.H.
pp
L.H.
ppp
poco rit.
L.H.
p più lento
pp
poco rit.
ppp
mp
Più mosso
scherzando

68
L.H.
L.H.
73
78
83
Prestissimo
pp
89
sfz

Wedding of the Winds

John T. Hall
1875–1954
Adapted by John Thompson

17
22
27
32
sf
sf
37

42
Con spirito
f
46
1.
2.
51
Brillante
f
56
1.
simile
61
2.
f

Animato
66
1.
ff
sf
sf
71
2.
76
Brillante
f
81
1.
86
2.

90
Con amore
mf
simile
98
1.
2.
poco rall.
107
f
114
poco rit.
119
Tempo di Valse
mf a tempo
simile

126
134
141
148
accel.
154
ff
sfz

To Oscar Rasbach

Artist's Life

Johann Strauss
1825–1899
Arranged by John Thompson

Tempo di Valse
31
allarg.
ff a tempo
37
sfz
42
sfz
espressivo
47
52
f
sfz

58
sfz
f
sfz
63
mp
allarg.
a tempo
68
74
79
f poco allarg.
a tempo

84
90
p
mf
95
f
mp poco allarg.
a tempo
100
105
sfz

110
8va
molto
115
121
127
R.H.
L.H.
dolce mp
133

139
molto ff
145
8va
ppp subito, like a music box
151
(8va)
sempre pp
157
(8va)
sfz
p
mf espressivo
164
mp

171
molto
allarg.
177
ff
183
sfz
sfz
espressivo
189
195
f

201
sfz
sfz
206
211
ff
217
ff
ff con brio
223
8va
cresc.
8va
sfz
sfz
ff

To John J. Cranley

Vienna Life

Johann Strauss
1825–1899
Arranged by John Thompson

29
34
41
mp scherz.
46
mp
51
f

56
L.H.
61
f
67
73
ff
79

85
91
p
mp
97
Meno mosso
espressivo
poco rit.
8va
a tempo
102
poco rit.
8va
107
a tempo
sfz
1.
mp

113
mf
marcato e sostenuto
119
125
131
Maestoso
ff
137
p scherz.

143
149
ff
155
ff
161
8va
p scherz.
167

173
8va
sempre animato
ff brillante
178
(8va)
183
sfz
mp
f
189
195

201
206
211
216
mp
221

226
231
ff
236
ff
242
ff
R.H.
248
8va
8va
f
sfz
ff

Waltz of the Flowers

from THE NUTCRACKER SUITE

Peter Ilyich Tchaikovsky
1840–1893
Arranged by John Thompson

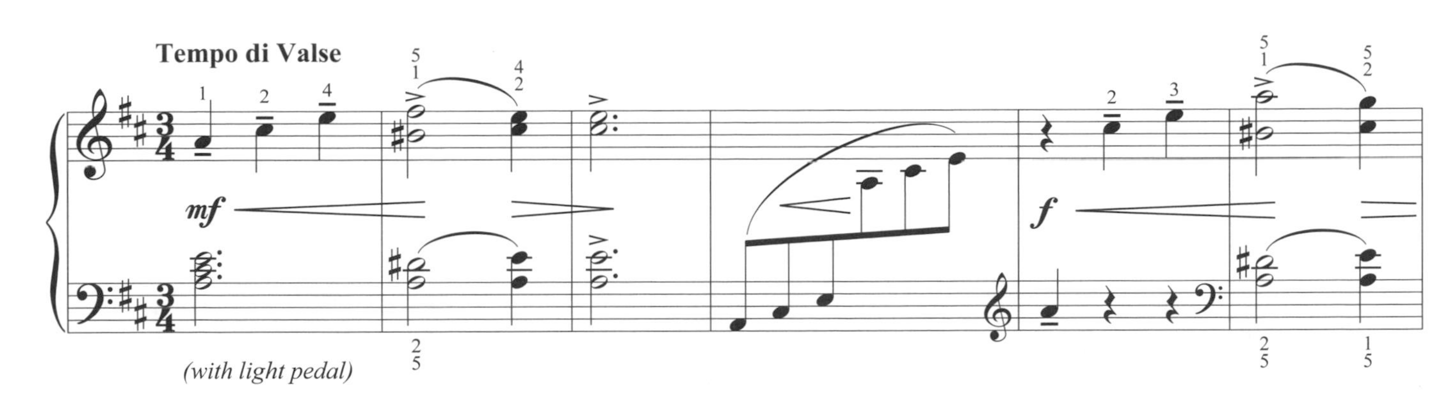

29
p
f
36
p
cresc.
mf
42
49
p
56
mf
f

62
69
cresc.
76
sfz
f
83
f
90
1.
2.
p

96
103
110
1.
2.
f
p
117
124

131
ff
137
143
150
cresc.
ff
157
poco rall.

164
p a tempo
171
p
cresc.
mf
177
184
mp
191

196
203
210
217
224

To Laurence B. Ellert

Paraphrase on
The Beautiful Blue Danube

Johann Strauss
1825–1899
Arranged by John Thompson

21
sfz
sfz
sfz
27
leggierissimo
mp
(with light pedal)
32
37
42

poco rit.
mf a tempo
pp
pp

sfz
p scherzando
f

109
ff
p sempre staccato
115
120
125
mf
rall.
132
pp molto tranquillo

139
1.
145
2.
poco rall.
cresc.
151
ff
ff
157
ff
163
1.
2.

170
sfz
sfz
mp
176
leggierissimo
182
188
194
poco rit.

200
Allegro
a tempo
f
ff
accel. poco a poco
206
simile
212
cresc.
ff
217
brillante
R.H.
L.H.
222
8va
ff
ffz

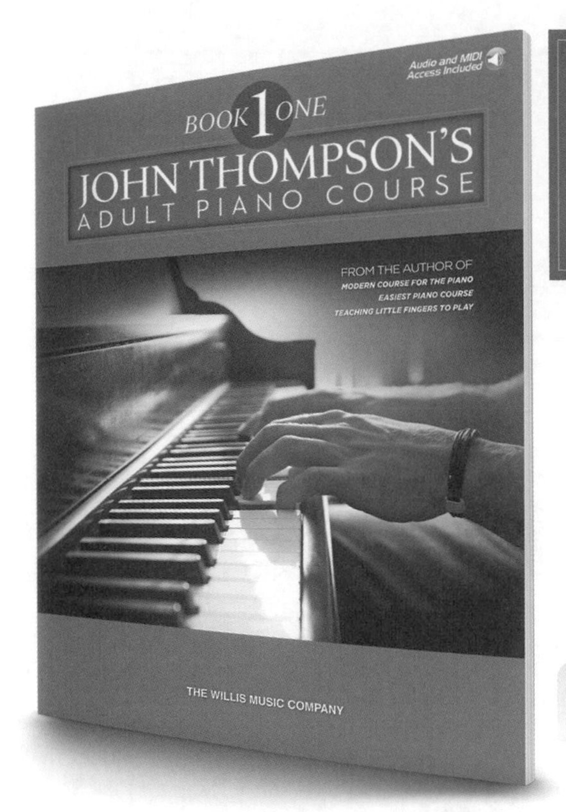

REDISCOVER JOHN THOMPSON'S ADULT PIANO COURSE

ADULT PIANO COURSE

Recently re-engraved and updated, *John Thompson's Adult Piano Course* was compiled with the mature student in mind. Adults have the same musical road to travel as the younger student, but the study material for mature students will differ slightly in content. Since these beloved books were written and arranged especially for adults, they contain a wonderful mix of classical arrangements, well-known folk-tunes and outstanding originals that many will find a pleasure to learn and play. Most importantly, the student is always encouraged to play as artistically and with as much musical understanding as possible. Access to orchestrations online is available and features two tracks for each piece: a demo track with the piano part, and one with just the accompaniment.

00122297 Book 1 – Book/Online Audio $14.99
00412639 Book 1 – Book Only $6.99
00122300 Book 2 – Book/Online Audio $14.99
00415763 Book 2 – Book Only $6.99

POPULAR PIANO SOLOS – JOHN THOMPSON'S ADULT PIANO COURSE

12 great arrangements that can be used on their own, or as a supplement to *John Thompson's Adult Piano Course*. Each book includes access to audio tracks online that be downloaded or streamed.

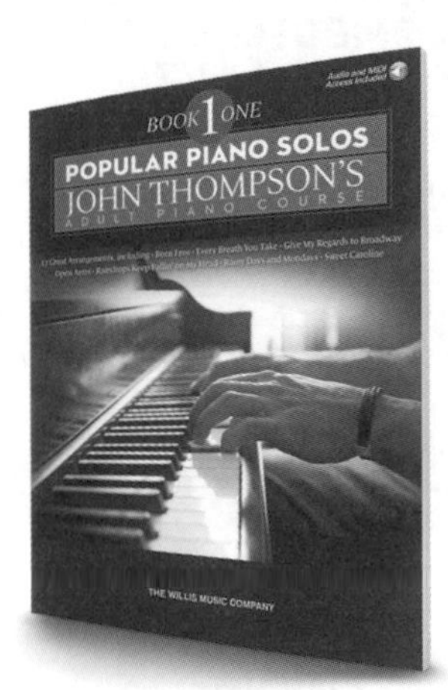

BOOK 1

arr. Carolyn Miller

Born Free • Can't Help Falling in Love • Every Breath You Take • Fields of Gold • Give My Regards to Broadway • A Groovy Kind of Love • My Life • Ob-La-Di, Ob-La-Da • Open Arms • Raindrops Keep Fallin' on My Head • Rainy Days and Mondays • Sweet Caroline.

00124215 Book/Online Audio $12.99

BOOK 2

arr. Eric Baumgartner & Glenda Austin

And So It Goes • Beauty and the Beast • Getting to Know You • Hey Jude • If My Friends Could See Me Now • Lollipop • My Favorite Things • Nadia's Theme • Strawberry Fields Forever • Sunrise, Sunset • Sway (Quien Será) • You Raise Me Up.

00124216 Book/Online Audio $12.99

Also Available, JOHN THOMPSON RECITAL SERIES:

SPIRITUALS

Intermediate to Advanced Level

Six excellent arrangements that are ideal for recital or church service. Titles: Deep River • Heav'n, Heav'n • I Want to Be Ready (Walk in Jerusalem, Jus' like John) • Nobody Knows De Trouble I've Seen • Short'nin' Bread • Swing Low, Sweet Chariot.

00137218 .... $6.99

THEME AND VARIATIONS

Intermediate to Advanced Level

Fantastic recital variations that are sure to impress: Chopsticks • Variations on Mary Had a Little Lamb • Variations on Chopin's C Minor Prelude • Three Blind Mice - Variations on the Theme • Variations on Twinkle, Twinkle, Little Star.

00137219 .... $8.99

WALTZES

Intermediate to Advanced Level

Excellent, virtuosic arrangements of famous romantic waltzes: Artist's Life (Strauss) • Paraphrase on the Beautiful Blue Danube (Strauss) • Dark Eyes (Russian Cabaret Song) • Vienna Life (Strauss) • Waltz of the Flowers (Tchaikovsky) • Wedding of the Winds (John T. Hall).

00137220 .... $8.99

Prices, contents, and availability subject to change without notice.

Please visit www.willispianomusic.com for these and hundreds of other classic and new publications from Willis Music.

0615